A Step-by-Step Guide
When a Love One Dies

By Maria Sare

16 Northolt Rd,
South Harrow, Harrow HA2 0ER,
United Kingdom

All rights reserved

Copyright © 2025 Maria Sare

ISBN (Paperback)
ISBN (Hardback)

Cover Design by London Book Publisher

No part of this publication may be reproduced, stored in a retrieval system, copied in any form or by any means, electronic, mechanical, photocopying, recording or otherwise transmitted without written permission from the publisher.

You must not circulate this book in any format. Under no circumstances will any blame or legal responsibility be held against the publisher, or author, for any damages, reparation, or monetary loss due to the information contained within this book, either directly or indirectly.

DISCLAIMER

The information contained in this guide, *A Step-by-Step Guide When a Loved One Dies*, is intended solely for informational and educational purposes. This guide aims to assist individuals in organising essential details following the death of a loved one; however, it is not a substitute for professional legal, financial, or medical advice. Readers are strongly encouraged to consult with qualified professionals regarding any specific matters requiring legal, medical, or financial expertise.

This guide may include personal and sensitive information. The Author and Publisher do not assume any responsibility for the use or misuse of the information contained within. It is the responsibility of the user to ensure that this guide is used ethically and appropriately, in accordance with applicable laws and regulations.

It is also important to highlight that, wherever this guide is stored, whether in a safe deposit box, a personal safe, or with a trusted individual, it is essential to make provisions for the transfer of this guide and all its contents to the next of kin or the executor of the estate upon the death of the individual. Ensuring that this information is readily accessible to those who will need it is a key step in facilitating the continuity of care and support for your loved ones.

By using this guide, you acknowledge that you understand and accept this disclaimer.

DEDICATION

To my beloved sisters Janet and Susan,
who are now on the other side

To my sister Lynn, who is very much alive,
and even during my own "death's door" experience
still managed to make me laugh

To my beloved husband Malcolm, whether I'm walking on the
Earth or in it, will be loved forever

About The Author

Maria Sare was originally from Aveley, South Ockendon, Essex.

She lived on the Kennington estate and is part of a large Irish family, being the youngest of eight.

She spent her years there until she met her first serious boyfriend at the age of 17. She went on to marry him and has been married for 36 years.

She has always cared about people, looking after several family members until they passed away.

She now lives a lovely, quiet life by the sea.

She has one son, Daniel, who is married to a lovely lady, Gemma, and she has three wonderful grandchildren: Danny, Savannah, and Hunter.

TABLE OF CONTENTS

END-OF-LIFE LUCIDITY PHENOMENON 1
My own personal experience 1
My death's door experience 2

INTRODUCTION 4

REGISTERING THE DEATH 5
Information you'll need to provide to the registrar: 5
Organise your documents: 5
Documents you should bring to the Registrar (if possible) 6
Once registered, you'll receive a death certificate. 6
Is there a will? 6
Is probate needed? 7
Apply For A Grant Of Probate 7
Owned Joint Assets 7
Informing Organisations And People 8
Template Letter 9
Example 10
Arranging The Funeral 11
The Time Between Death and The Funeral 12
The Funeral 12
Keep A Memory Box 13

DAY AFTER FUNERAL 14
From hectic to static what do I do now? 14
Lonely 14
Contact Your Local Council 15
Bereavement Services 15
Specialised Support 15
Financial Discounts 15
Template Letter for Discount 17

AUTHOR'S NOTE 18

END-OF-LIFE LUCIDITY PHENOMENON

MY OWN PERSONAL EXPERIENCE

The experience of witnessing a loved one's final days often involves a complex emotional landscape, marked by anticipation, grief, and sometimes, unexpected moments of clarity.

One of my experiences, and I have witnessed a few, was with my father. A sudden awakening from his unconscious state, his unexpected communication with me, and his requests, all occurring hours before his death. It gave me hope. I thought he wouldn't die. He suddenly sat up after being unconscious for days, asking me what was wrong and why I was sitting in his bedroom.

He then told me he was hungry and wanted a cheesecake, something he had never eaten in his life. My sister, who was staying with me at the time, thinking our father was going to die, rushed to the shops to buy him a cheesecake. On her return from the local shop, with cheesecake in hand, she entered the bedroom and he almost snatched it from her. Rejecting the offer of a plate, he took the bag containing the cheesecake and scoffed it as if he had been starved. He asked for a drink.

He then asked why my sister was there. We looked at each other, very puzzled and very relieved, thinking he was going to be okay. My sister, after staying with me for several days, was going to return to her own home that day, convinced he was okay and not on the long, unknown journey at all.

We were happy, we were relieved, this was a miracle, we thought. We were on such a high. The emotional impact this event had on me will stay forever, but it has prepared me in a way to look for these signs in others so I am not fooled again and can try to prepare for the unexpected, just to ease the false hope.

My father, after scoffing the cheesecake, laid down and never woke again. He died a few hours later.

I do wonder now, do loved ones do this so you can have a final conversation? Or are they just filling their bellies for the long unknown journey that lies ahead?

MY DEATH'S DOOR EXPERIENCE

This experience, I ironically felt myself, whilst writing this book and the book being with the London Book Publishers, at the editing stage.

I became very ill and literally physically sick for several days, being bedridden, in and out of sleep. Very weak. And very scared that I was on death's door. I felt I was on death's door. I hoped I was wrong. I had never been ill like that in my life.

At first, I thought it was food poisoning, but that was ruled out. I could not take any more of the sickness, so three days in, my husband called the NHS helpline, and in turn, they called the ambulance. Off I was taken to hospital. I must thank all the ambulance crew and the hospital—they were absolutely fantastic. I feel Colchester Hospital in Essex (A&E) deserves a mention alongside all the ambulance crew that took care of me.

I had every test, but nothing was really coming back positive. I was put on a drip and intravenous antibiotics. I felt better and was discharged the same day, only to return home, and the sickness started again.

Again, in and out of sleep. Not eating anything. The thought of food I could not bear to see or smell. Then, to my astonishment, I woke and wanted a barbecue chicken pizza. I was scared. Then I wanted an ice lolly (something I do not really eat). I was scared. Despite the pain I was in, I did not want to die. That was yesterday.

And today, I feel good. I'm hoping that in my personal experience, I was not getting ready for my own "unknown" journey.

I heard that people see a bright light before their passing and they start to walk into it. My thoughts at this stage were: "Don't you dare show me that light."

I really feel I dodged death this time.

INTRODUCTION

Dealing with the death of a loved one is indeed one of the most challenging experiences, and the administrative burden that follows can feel overwhelming.

I offer within my book to simplify things and provide assistance with template letters.

Having clear, straightforward templates can be a huge help in navigating these necessary steps.

REGISTERING THE DEATH

This is one of the first things that needs to happen. In the UK, you generally need to register the death within five days. You'll receive a Medical Certificate of Cause of Death from the doctor or hospital, which you'll need to take to the local Registrar of Marriages, Births and Deaths.

(YOU MAY WANT TO CALL AHEAD IN CASE INCASE YOU NEED AN APPOINTMENT).

INFORMATION YOU'LL NEED TO PROVIDE TO THE REGISTRAR:

- Full name and surname of the deceased (including any previous names, like a maiden name)
- Date and place of death
- Main address
- Date and place of birth
- Occupation
- If the deceased was married or in a civil partnership, their spouse's full name, date of birth, and occupation.
- If the deceased was receiving a State Pension or other benefits.

ORGANISE YOUR DOCUMENTS:

Try and obtain a folder to keep everything relating to the death together. It is also advisable to get some large sized envelopes preferably A4, as documents will not need folding. You'll also need:

- A book of stamps
- A pen and pencil, (I suggest a pencil, as you can tick off in the book what documents you have obtained)

DOCUMENTS YOU SHOULD BRING TO THE REGISTRAR (IF POSSIBLE)

- Medical Certificate of Cause of Death
- Birth Certificate of the deceased
- Marriage or civil partnership certificate (if applicable)
- NHS medical card/number
- Proof of your own identity and address (e.g., bank statement/utility bill)

ONCE REGISTERED, YOU'LL RECEIVE A DEATH CERTIFICATE.

At this point, I advise getting several death certificates, as when informing other organisations like the banks everyone will request a certified copy and will not accept photocopies.

Also request a **Certificate for Burial or Cremation** (Green Form); the funeral director will request this from you to proceed with the funeral.

Is There A Will?
When someone has died and they have a will, the process that follows is called probate.

- Locate the original will
- Identify the executors (they will apply for probate)
- Ascertain the value of the estate

- Pay for the funeral.
- Funeral costs are usually paid from the deceased's estate.

Banks will often release funds directly from the deceased's account for funeral expenses if a funeral director's invoice is provided.

Is Probate Needed?
- If property was in the deceased's sole name, probate is likely to be needed, as property cannot be sold or transferred without it.
- If the deceased had over £30,000 in the bank in their sole name or owned shares probate is needed.
- Probate is generally needed to deal with Premium Bonds after the holder's death if the total value of the deceased's assets held with National Savings and Investments (NS&I) (including Premium Bonds) exceeds £5,000.00.
- If the total value is £5,000 or less probate may not be needed.

NS&I provides a claim form to be completed by the executor or administrator to inform them of the deceased's holdings and to indicate whether they wish for the bonds to remain in the prize draw for up to 12 months or to be cashed in sooner.

APPLY FOR A GRANT OF PROBATE

- Online application: https://www.gov.uk/applying-for-probate)
- Forms: The executors will need to complete specific forms, including the probate application form (PA1) and potentially inheritance tax forms (e.g., IHT205 for simple estates or IHT400 for more complex ones).

Owned Joint Assets
Probate is unlikely to be needed because these assets will simply transfer to the surviving owner

Informing Organisations And People
- GOV.UK Tell Us Once (you can do this online)
- Banks and building societies
- Premium bonds
- Utility companies
- Insurance companies
- Pension providers
- Employer
- Landlord/mortgage provider
- Credit card companies/Loan providers
- Dentist, GP, Optician
- Subscription Services (Newspapers, Amazon, Netflix, Magazines etc.)
- Passport Office: To cancel passport
- DVLA
- Email providers: so account can be closed
- Hairdressers, barbers, nail salons etc. (Your loved one may have pre-booked an appointment). It's quite upsetting to get a call to ask where your loved one is as they haven't turned up for their appointment).
- Fishing Licence

You can also request a credit report, which will show all details of the account history. It provides a detailed history of financial behaviour. You can obtain a credit report for a deceased person, but it requires specific authorisation and documentation. The executor or administrator of the deceased's estate can request the report from the credit reference agencies (CRAs) like Experian, TransUnion, and Equifax.

TEMPLATE LETTER

A sample of a template letter follows. You can either type or handwrite it. Simply omit the company and account details, and once copied, fill in the relevant information. If you have no access to a computer, a handwritten letter will suffice. Again leave gaps where the information should go and photocopy it as many times as you need.

Example
YOUR NAME
YOUR ADDRESS
YOUR PHONE NUMBER
YOUR EMAIL ADDRESS

DATE

SUBJECT: NOTIFICATION OF DEATH

I am writing to inform you of the death of (Deceased full name), who died on (Date of Death). Their date of birth was (Deceased date of birth) and their last address was (Deceased last address).

They held an account with your company. Their reference/account number was (......................)

If you have other account numbers or reference numbers, you can add them here.

I have enclosed an original copy of the Death Certificate.

Please inform me of any outstanding payments or benefits that may be due.

Thank you for your time and assistance.

Yours sincerely,
Sign
Print name

ARRANGING THE FUNERAL

All funeral directors will provide advice and support when you are arranging a funeral.

Check to see if the deceased had made a will, as they may have specified their choice of funeral director and/or their last wishes.

If no will exists, it is your personal choice whom to choose. Friends or relatives may even suggest a funeral director they have used in the past. Keep in mind, if you plan to visit your loved one at the funeral home, a local one may be more convenient for you.

Funeral directors are very special people, who truly care about your loved one. They take their time with you, so do not be afraid if you are feeling inconsolable or finding it hard to cope. They will help you feel calm, and there's no rush. Take your time.

One thing to consider is that they will ask you for clothing for the deceased. It might help to bring a photograph of the deceased, as this will guide them in preparing the body for viewing. This process is known as embalming, and they will aim to make your loved one look as close to how they appeared before their passing.

Please note that this may not always be possible, depending on the cause of death.

Take your time with the clothing; there's no rush. You may have seen your loved one in a favourite colour/ suit/ dress, for example.

The process of selecting clothing can feel very overwhelming and upsetting. So, take breaks, and return to it when you can.

It might give you time to think: "Oh, she always looked lovely in those earrings, or he always wore that watch." You may want to dress them in these special items, and that's fine too.

This is your final goodbye, so make it feel right for you.

Take your time. You want it to be special and it will be.

The Time Between Death and The Funeral
Many people will visit during this time, and there will be a lot of tea and coffee making.

When help is offered, take it. If someone asks if there's anything they can do to help, say "YES."

If you have many visitors at one time, ask one person to make the tea and coffee. They really won't mind.

Make sure you're sitting and resting. The death of a loved one takes a significant toll on you.

Remember, after the funeral, you may notice that many of those visitors won't come around again. So, take help when you can.

THE FUNERAL

Think about yourself and your loved one only.

- Wear comfortable shoes, and have lots of tissues in every pocket, you'll be glad you did, it also saves you from fumbling around during the funeral.
- People don't expect you to engage in full-blown conversations. If you don't feel like talking, just politely excuse yourself by saying you need to use the bathroom or offer another excuse. No

one will be offended. This is an important day for both you and your loved one.
- Ask someone to collect the cards from the flowers (the funeral director can do this if you ask). Keep one or two copies of the order of service.
- Take a flower from your wreath, or any flower that catches your eye.

Keep A Memory Box

Creating a memory box can be incredibly helpful for processing grief at your own pace. The day of the funeral can be overwhelming, and it's hard for everything to sink in.

A memory box allows you to collect items that remind you of your loved one and revisit them when you feel ready. It creates a space for reflection and remembrance that you can engage with at your own pace, long after the immediate events of the funeral.

Flower cards, orders of service, a fresh flower—anything that reminds you of the day. You can put these in a memory box.

Ask a relative to take photos of the flowers. You may not want them on the day but in the future, when talking about the funeral, you may wish to look back and see how beautiful it was. Although the sadness will remain forever, these memories can bring comfort.

In time, you will learn to live with the situation in time. Trust me.

DAY AFTER FUNERAL

FROM HECTIC TO STATIC WHAT DO I DO NOW?

It's been a hectic time; it's now all so quiet. Although letters are being returned from the banks and organisations, there's still paperwork to sort. You may look around and see items, clothes, photos—they make you upset. That's fine. Crying is normal. Shouting is normal. Screaming is normal. Anger is normal. Every emotion you will go through. All are normal; that's part of the healing process.

It will get better. It will never go away, but in time, you will learn to ease the pain in your own unique way. There are no rights or wrongs. My best piece of advice is, if you're thinking of clearing out everything, that's fine. But please keep a memory box. Take one, two, three, or fifty-three items, pop them in a box. An item of clothing, or a pair of slippers. A hat, scarf, shirt, or blouse. Pop them in the memory box. Put the box under the bed or on top of the wardrobe. You can then go back to them, sometime in the future when you feel up to it. If you discard everything, you may feel upset in the future, that you didn't keep anything.

Lonely

It may feel so lonely now and you might feel like part of you is missing. Try to keep busy. Join local groups. Things you have never done before—just join, go along; if you don't like it, don't go back. But you will see people. People who are more than likely in the same position as yourself. You will make new friends.

Try saying yes to everything that's offered. From a cup of tea down the road at a neighbours to a beer, wine, or your favourite tipple in the local pub. Go along, people do understand. Do not be afraid to get upset. Talk to people. Your local council should have a list of local events in your area. Volunteer in a charity shop. Seeing and talking to people is a great thing.

If you cannot see the light at the end of the tunnel, please seek professional help.

Samaritans are a good organisation and they are open 24 hours a day. Find out your local number and write it down. Keep it safe.

Contact Your Local Council

Bereavement Services
Many councils provide services like burial grounds, crematoria, and assistance with funerals for those who die with no one to make arrangements.

Specialised Support
Some councils offer more specialised bereavement support, for different types of bereavement (e.g., suicide, drug-related deaths), and for young people and children.

It's best to check with your local council as services can vary.

Financial Discounts

If you now live alone after the death of your loved one it is a good idea to contact your local council and all your utility companies. Some provide discounts for single occupancy.

The council assumes that there are two adults living in your home. If you are the only adult living in your home (as your main residence), you are entitled to a 25% single person discount on your Council Tax bill. You might also be able to claim a discount if you live with someone under 18, if you are a student, if you live with a student, if you're a carer, or if there are major changes to your home's value. The template following can be sent to your local council and utility suppliers to enquire if you are entitled to a discount.

Template Letter for Discount
YOUR NAME
YOUR ADDRESS
YOUR PHONE NUMBER
YOUR EMAIL ADDRESS

DATE

SUBJECT: NOTIFICATION OF DEATH

I am writing to inform you of the death of (Deceased's full name), who died on (Date of Death). Their date of birth was (Deceased's date of birth) and their last address was (same as above).

I now live at this address on my own (or your personal circumstances), and I am enquiring if I can get any discount due to my situation.

If you have account numbers or any reference numbers, you can add them here.

I have enclosed an original copy of the Death Certificate.

Please inform me what I need to do.

Thank you for your time and assistance.

Yours sincerely,
Sign
Print name

Author's Note

I have been through an incredibly challenging time, experiencing multiple close family deaths within short periods and bearing the brunt of the practical arrangements myself. My desire is to help others navigate this difficult process by sharing my experiences and writing this book.

Losing someone is incredibly difficult, and it's true that many people feel lost when it comes to the practicalities and emotional challenges that follow. My book is designed to guide people through such a tough time, and hopefully make a significant difference.

I send my love and hugs to each and every one of you.

God Bless!

www.ingramcontent.com/pod-product-compliance
Lightning Source LLC
Chambersburg PA
CBHW061227070526
44584CB00029B/4021